POLLEN

Darwin's 130 Year Prediction

Written by Darcy Pattison & Illustrated by Peter Willis

Moments in Science

POLLEN: Darwin's 130 Year Prediction
Written by Darcy Pattison
Illustrated by Peter Willis

Mims House would like to thank Dr.
Wasserthal for use of his photograph.
Wasserthal, L.T. (1997) Bot. Acta. 110,
343-359.

Publisher's Cataloging-in-Publication data

Names: Pattison, Darcy, author. | Willis,
Peter, illustrator.
Title: Pollen : Darwin's 130 year prediction
/ written by Darcy Pattison and illustrated
by Peter Willis.
Description: Little Rock, AR: Mims
House, 2019.
Identifiers: ISBN 978-1-62944-119-1
(Hardcover) | 978-1-62944-120-7 (pbk.) |
978-1-62944-121-4 (ebook)
Subjects: LCSH Darwin, Charles, 1809-1882--Juvenile literature. | Discoveries
in science--History--Juvenile literature. | Pollination by insects--Juvenile literature.
| Orchids--Juvenile literature. | Lepidoptera--Juvenile literature. | Moths--Juve-
nile literature. | Plants—Evolution--Juvenile literature. | Pollinators—Evolution--Juvenile
literature. | Life sciences--History--Juvenile literature. | BISAC JUVENILE NON-
FICTION / Science & Nature / Discoveries | JUVENILE NONFICTION /
Science & Nature / History of Science | JUVENILE NONFICTION / Science
& Nature / Flowers & Plants | JUVENILE NONFICTION / Animals / Insects,
Spiders, etc.
Classification: LCC Q180.55.D57 .P38 2019 | DDC 500--dc23

Sometimes, science takes a long time.

On January 25, 1862, a box arrived at the home of the British scientist, Charles Darwin. When Darwin opened it, he saw. . .

CHARLES DARWIN
ENGLAND

orchids!

Laelia anceps

Odontoglossum pulchellum

Odontoglossum bictoniense

Zygopetalum crinitum

Angraecum sesquipedale

The star orchid from Madagascar

←

YOU C[...]

A star orchid from Madagascar surprised Darwin. It had a glossy six-rayed flower, like stars formed of snow-white wax. Its nectary measured 11.5 inches (29.2 cm) long. A nectary is the place where flowers make nectar, the sweet liquid that insects and birds eat.

Darwin realized the unusually long nectary was a scientific mystery. How was this flower pollinated?

PAN BOOKS LTD : LONDON

Pollination means that the flower's pollen is carried from one flower to another.

When a flower is pollinated, it develops seeds which can grow new plants.

For some flowers, the wind blows pollen from plant to plant.

But for some flowers, insects pollinate the flowers.

An insect flies to the flower to drink nectar.

As the insect brushes against the flower, pollen sticks to the insect.

When it moves to the next flower, the pollen brushes off the insect onto the new flower.

When Darwin studied the Madagascar star orchid, he wondered how an insect could drink its nectar.

Hhhhmm

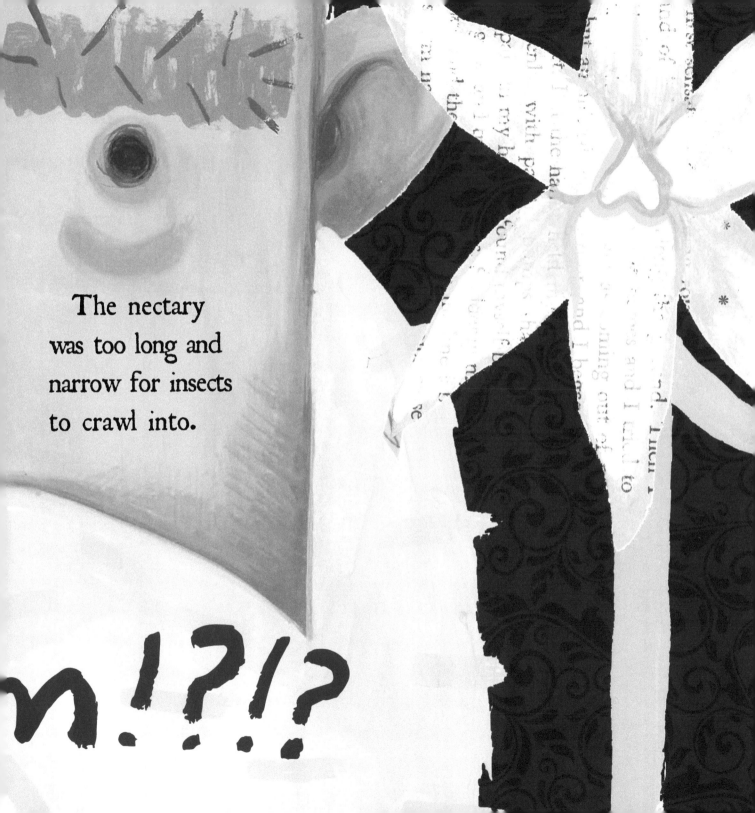

The nectary
was too long and
narrow for insects
to crawl into.

n.!?!?

Darwin tried pushing bristles and needles into the nectary opening but couldn't pick up any pollen.

FINALLY!

he thought about how moths pollinated flowers. Moths use a proboscis (pro-BOSS-kss) like a straw to drink nectar.

Darwin pushed a thin glass tube into the orchid's nectary. Pollen attached to the glass, and Darwin could pollinate another flower.

Like a detective figuring out a mystery, Darwin made an amazing guess or prediction.

The orchid with a long nectary grew somewhere on the island of Madagascar, he said. That meant somewhere in Madagascar, there must be a giant moth with an eleven-inch long proboscis.

You couldn't have one without the other, he reasoned. The moth and the orchid would depend on each other. The orchid would give nectar, or food, to the moth, and the moth would collect pollen to pollinate another orchid so more orchids could grow.

However, no one had seen such a moth. When Charles Darwin died in 1882, still, no one had seen a giant moth with an eleven-inch long proboscis.

The moth would pollinate another orchid.

Twenty one years later, in 1903,

two entomologists, or insect scientists, published a new book about moths. Baron Rothschild and Karl Jordan described a new Madagascar hawk moth, (Xanthopan morgani praedicta | zan-THOOP-an mor-GAN-ee pray-DICT-uh). It had a very long proboscis that was coiled at the base of the moth's head until needed. When it needed to drink nectar, the moth unrolled the proboscis.

← 6 INCHES →

But Darwin was wrong about one thing. The hawk moth was big, but not as big as he expected. Its wingspan measured only about five or six inches.

But the mystery wasn't totally solved. It seemed like the star orchid and hawk moth should go together. But no one had seen the hawk moth pollinate the star orchid until. . .

In 1992, German entomologist, Lutz Thilo Wasserthal, Ph.D decided to try to photograph the elusive moth at the orchid. He set up a flight tent. He gathered star orchids from rocky slopes and placed them inside. The moths were nocturnal, only active at night. So Wasserthal set up night vision cameras and infrared illumination, equipment that let him take night pictures.

All they needed were moths. But the hawk moths were rare. During the six-week stay in Madagascar, Wasserthal was only lucky enough to catch two of them.

With everything set up, Wasserthal released
the two hawk moths into the flight cage.
The air was filled with the aromatic spicy
scent from the flowers.

The scientists waited, then finally. . .

nectar

had po

the

. . . a hawk moth appeared and hovered in front of the star orchid. To drink, the moth unfurled its proboscis and inserted it into the nectary. It grabbed hold of the flower and shoved the proboscis down to the nectar. When it came away, the moth had pollen on the proboscis to carry to the next flower.

It only took about six seconds.

Here's the reality about science: sometimes progress can take years. Darwin made observations, tested his ideas, and made a prediction. Later, Rothschild and Jordan catalogued new species of moths. They assumed they had found Darwin's moth, but they couldn't prove it. 130 years after Darwin's prediction, Wasserthal made the hard journey to Madagascar to prove them all right. Progress in science needs predictions, observations over a long period of time, and sometimes, a bit of luck.

MORGAN'S SPHINX MOTH OR HAWKMOTH

Xanthopan morganii praedicta (zan-THOOP-an mor-GAN-ee pray-DICT-uh)

This is a large moth found in eastern Africa. Its wingspan is 5-6 inches (12-15 cm) wide. To eat, the moth sucks nectar through its proboscis, or tongue, which is a hollow tube like an elephant's trunk. It can be 12-18 inches (30-45 cm) long. When it's not in use, the proboscis is coiled under its head. The moths have narrow wings and streamlined abdomens. When they feed, sphinx moths hover like hummingbirds. They often move rapidly from side to side, which is called swing-hovering. Morgan's Sphinx moth is a native of Madagascar. Little is known about its life cycle.

Madagascar Rain Forests

The orchid and moth are both native to Madagascar, an island in the Indian Ocean just off the eastern coast of South Africa. In the last 60 years, it's lost 44% of its forest cover. This means the orchids and moths are losing habitat.

MADAGASCAR STAR ORCHID

Angraecum sesquipedale (An-GRAY-uh-Koom Ses-QUIP-ah-DOLL-eh) is an orchid which is native to Madagascar. Other names for this flower include Christmas orchid, comet orchid and the Star of Bethlehem orchid. The scientific name *Angraecum* comes from a Malay word for orchid, Angurek. The specific name comes from Latin: *sesqui* means one-and-a-half and *pedalis* means one-foot-long. This refers to the 10-12 inch (25-30 cm) nectary. Orchids don't grow in soil or dirt. Instead, an orchid's roots attach to tree trunks, or sometimes to rocks. The plant can grow up to 36 inches (1 meter) tall. Long, dark, grey-green leaves are 15 inches (40 cm) long. It blooms from June to September. When it flowers, it has 1-3 star-shaped blooms. It starts as a green flower but changes to a creamy white. It's threatened by loss of habitat and because it's collected for sale to orchid lovers.

SOURCE

Arditti, J., Elliott, J., Kitching I.J. and Wasserthal, L.T. (2012): 'Good Heavens what insect can suck it' - Charles Darwin, Angraecum sesquipedale and Xanthopan morganii praedicta. Botanical Journal of the Linnean Society 2012, 160, 403-432. https://doi.org/10.1111/j.1095-8339.2012.01250.x

Emails with Lutz Thilo Wasserthal, Ph.D. January 2018.

CHARLES DARWIN

Charles Darwin (February 12, 1809 - April 19, 1882) was a naturalist, geologist and biologist best known for his book, *The Origin of the Species*. He suggested that all life came from a common ancestor, which we call evolution. However, he studied and wrote about many other topics, including how orchids are fertilized, coral reefs, earthworms, fossils, and plants that eat insects. In 1862, Darwin predicted that the Madagascar star orchid would be fertilized by a giant moth. He suggested that the moth and orchid had co-evolved. Five years later, in 1867, scientist Alfred Russel Wallace supported Darwin's prediction, but instead of a giant moth, he predicted it would be a sphinx moth with a long, coiled proboscis.

LUTZ THILO WASSERTHAL, Ph.D.

Lutz Thilo Wasserthal, Ph.D. (August 22, 1940 -) is a German entomologist, or insect scientist. He's been a university professor since 1983. After his trip to Madagascar in 1992, he developed Darwin's ideas about co-evolution of the moth and orchid. Large huntsmen spiders are often attracted by flower-visiting moths which they recognize because of the vibrations from their wings. The spiders try to jump and catch the moths. Wasserthal suggested that the hawk moths evolved a longer proboscis to escape the jumping spiders or other predators. This meant that the flowers adapted to the moths, rather than co-evolving. Wasserthal also studied how insects breathe, how butterflies keep their body temperatures even, and the life cycle of butterflies.

GLOSSARY

Orchid - a flowering plant that grows above the ground; its roots are not in soil. Orchids are known for their showy flowers.

Nectar - sweet liquid made by plants. Nectar is food for insects and birds. When they come to drink the nectar, they pollinate the flower.

Nectary - the part of the flower that makes nectar

Pollen - the flower part that is needed to create seeds and more flowers

Pollinate - to carry pollen to the stigma of a flower where it will create seeds

Moth - a winged insect. Unlike butterflies, they have feathery antennae and are usually nocturnal, which means they come out at night.

Entomologist - a scientist who studies insects.

Above: This is a close-up photo of the coiled proboscis of a hawk moth. Like an elephant's trunk, the moth uses the proboscis to suck up the plant's nectar. Photo by Lutz Thilo Wasserthal, Ph.D.

Right: This is the original 1992 photo taken by Lutz Thilo Wasserthal, Ph.D. Notice that the proboscis has been uncoiled so the moth can insert it into the plant's nectary.

Wasserthal. L. T: Bot.Acta. 110 (1997), 343-359

OTHER BOOKS IN THE
MOMENTS IN SCIENCE COLLECTION:

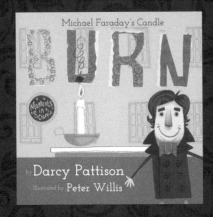

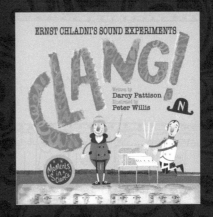

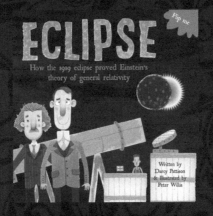